I0011980

Excel 101: A Beginner's Guide to Mastering Microsoft Excel

Copyright (c) 2023 by James C. Hammond

All rights reserved. No part of this book may be reproduced in any form or by any electronic or mechanical means, including information storage and retrieval systems, without permission in writing from the publisher, except by a reviewer who may quote brief passages in a review.

Table of Contents

Chapter 1: Introduction to Excel

Microsoft Excel is a powerful and versatile spreadsheet application used by millions of people worldwide for various purposes, from simple data organization to complex financial modeling. In this introductory chapter, we will embark on a journey to acquaint you with the fundamental aspects of Microsoft Excel and its significance in today's data-driven world.

1.1 What is Microsoft Excel?

Microsoft Excel is a part of the Microsoft Office suite of productivity software. It is primarily designed for creating, managing, and analyzing data in a tabular format. With Excel, you can:

• Create spreadsheets: Excel allows you to create structured grids, commonly known as worksheets, where you can input and organize your data efficiently.

• Perform calculations: It offers a wide range of mathematical and statistical functions to manipulate your data, making it a valuable tool for businesses, scientists, and students alike.

• Visualize data: Excel enables you to transform raw data into visually appealing charts and graphs, making it easier to interpret and present your findings.

1.2 Why Learn Excel?

Excel is not merely a spreadsheet program; it's a fundamental tool that has wide-ranging applications in diverse industries. Here are a few compelling reasons to learn Excel:

1. Career Advancement: Proficiency in Excel is a highly sought-after skill in the job market. Many employers require Excel skills for various positions, ranging from administrative roles to data analysis and finance.

2. Efficient Data Management: Excel provides a structured and organized way to handle data. Whether you're organizing a personal budget or managing company finances, Excel simplifies the process.

3. Data Analysis: Excel's functions and tools can help you analyze data and draw meaningful insights. This is invaluable for making informed decisions, both professionally and personally.

4. Time Savings: As you become proficient, Excel can automate repetitive tasks and save you considerable time. Learning how to use Excel effectively can significantly boost your productivity.

5. Problem Solving: Excel is a problem-solving tool. It allows you to model various scenarios, perform 'what-if' analyses, and find solutions to complex issues.

1.3 Structure of This Book

In "Excel 101: A Beginner's Guide to Mastering Microsoft Excel," we have structured the content to ensure a gradual and comprehensive learning experience. Each chapter is designed to build upon the knowledge gained in the previous one, equipping you with the skills needed to become a proficient Excel user.

The subsequent chapters will cover topics such as the Excel interface, creating workbooks, data entry, formulas, and functions, among others, in a step-by-step manner. By the end of this book, you will have a solid foundation in Excel and be capable of handling various spreadsheet-related tasks.

1.4 Getting Started

Before delving into the practical aspects of Excel in the following chapters, it's essential to ensure you have access to Excel. If you don't already have it installed, we will guide you on how to acquire the software and provide an overview of its user interface in the upcoming chapter.

In conclusion, this chapter has set the stage for your journey to master Microsoft Excel. You've learned what Excel is, why it's important, and what to expect from this book. Now, let's move on to Chapter 2, where we'll guide you through the process of getting started with Excel and navigating its user interface.

Chapter 2: Getting Started with Excel

In this chapter, we take the first step into the world of Microsoft Excel. We'll guide you through the process of acquiring the software if you don't already have it and introduce you to the Excel interface. Familiarizing yourself with the Excel interface is essential for efficiently navigating and utilizing this powerful spreadsheet application.

2.1 Acquiring Microsoft Excel

Before you can start working with Excel, you need to have it installed on your computer. There are a few ways to obtain Microsoft Excel:

Microsoft 365 Subscription:

- Microsoft 365 is a subscription service that includes Excel and other Office applications like Word, PowerPoint, and Outlook. You can purchase a subscription, which typically includes the latest version of Excel, and access it online or install it on your computer.

Standalone Microsoft Excel:

- You can also purchase a standalone version of Microsoft Excel. These are one-time purchases, and you'll have access to the specific version you buy without ongoing subscription fees.

Free Alternatives:

• For those on a budget or looking for free alternatives, consider options like Microsoft Excel Online (a web-based version of Excel) or open-source alternatives like LibreOffice Calc and Google Sheets.

2.2 Exploring the Excel Interface

When you open Microsoft Excel, you'll be greeted by the Excel interface. Let's break down the key components:

2.2.1 Ribbon:

The Ribbon is the horizontal bar at the top of the Excel window. It's divided into tabs, each containing groups of related commands. You'll find essential functions like "File," "Home," "Insert," "Page Layout," "Formulas," "Data," "Review," and "View" on the Ribbon.

2.2.2 Quick Access Toolbar:

This small toolbar is located above the Ribbon and provides shortcuts to frequently used commands. You can customize it to include the functions you use most often.

2.2.3 Workbook and Worksheets:

A workbook is the main file in Excel. It can contain multiple worksheets (also referred to as sheets), each represented as a tab at the bottom of the Excel window. Worksheets are where you enter and manipulate data.

2.2.4 Cells:

Cells are the individual rectangular boxes within a worksheet. They are identified by a combination of letters and numbers, such as "A1," "B2," or "C3." You enter and manipulate data within cells.

2.2.5 Formula Bar:

The Formula Bar, located just below the Ribbon, is where you enter and edit formulas and data. When you click on a cell, its content appears in the Formula Bar.

2.2.6 Name Box:

The Name Box is found to the left of the Formula Bar. It displays the address or name of the currently selected cell.

2.2.7 Status Bar:

The Status Bar, located at the bottom of the Excel window, provides information about the current state of your workbook, such as the sum, average, and count of selected cells.

2.3 Your First Steps

Now that you're acquainted with the Excel interface, it's time to take your first steps. Open Excel, explore the Ribbon and its tabs, create a new workbook, and start entering data into a worksheet. You might want to experiment with basic formatting options, such as changing fonts and cell colors.

Remember, mastering Excel is a step-by-step process, and these fundamental skills will serve as the foundation for more advanced concepts and operations in the chapters that   follow.

Chapter 3: Understanding the Excel Interface

In this chapter, we will delve deeper into the Microsoft Excel interface, focusing on essential elements and features that enable efficient navigation and utilization of this powerful spreadsheet software. A solid understanding of the interface is crucial for any Excel user, as it forms the basis for all your spreadsheet operations.

3.1 The Ribbon Revisited

The Ribbon, that prominent horizontal bar at the top of the Excel window, deserves a more in-depth exploration. It's divided into several tabs, each offering a specific set of functions. Here are some of the most commonly used tabs and their purposes:

- Home Tab: This tab contains everyday commands for formatting, styling, and editing your data. You'll find options for font formatting, cell alignment, and basic data manipulation here.

- Insert Tab: The Insert tab is where you go to add various elements to your workbook, such as charts, pictures, tables, or hyperlinks. It's crucial for enhancing your data presentation.

- Formulas Tab: If you want to perform calculations in Excel, the Formulas tab is your go-to. It houses a wide array of functions and formulas that allow you to work with numerical and textual data effectively.

- Data Tab: When working with data sets, the Data tab provides tools for sorting, filtering, and managing your data. You can also use it for importing and exporting data from external sources.

- Page Layout Tab: For those who need to print or format their worksheets for professional reports, the

Page Layout tab offers options for page setup, printing, and worksheet design.

•   View Tab: This tab controls the view settings of your workbook. You can switch between different views, such as Normal, Page Layout, and Page Break Preview.

3.2 Customizing the Quick Access Toolbar

Efficiency in Excel often comes from personalizing the environment to suit your needs. The Quick Access Toolbar is a versatile tool for this purpose. You can customize it by adding buttons for commands you frequently use, making them easily accessible from the top of the Excel window.

To customize the Quick Access Toolbar, follow these steps:

1.   Click the dropdown arrow on the right side of the Quick Access Toolbar.

2.   Select the commands you want to add from the menu that appears.

3.3 Workbook and Worksheet Essentials

Excel revolves around the concept of workbooks and worksheets. Here's what you need to know about them:

• Workbook: A workbook is the main Excel file. It's where you enter, organize, and store data. You can have multiple workbooks open simultaneously.

• Worksheets: Worksheets are the individual tabs you see at the bottom of your Excel window. They are part of a workbook and are used to separate and organize data. You can add, delete, and rename worksheets as needed.

3.4 Saving Your Work

Now that you're becoming more familiar with the Excel interface, it's important to understand how to save your work. To save your workbook, follow these steps:

1.   Click the "File" tab on the Ribbon.

2.   Select "Save" or "Save As" to choose the save location and format.

Regularly saving your work is crucial to avoid data loss in case of unexpected disruptions.

3.5 Your Journey Continues

With a deeper understanding of the Excel interface, you're

well on your way to mastering this versatile spreadsheet software. Your ability to navigate the Ribbon, customize the Quick Access Toolbar, and grasp the fundamentals of workbooks and worksheets is setting the stage for more advanced Excel skills.

In the following chapters, we'll delve into data entry, formatting, basic formulas, and functions, empowering you to create and manage your data effectively. Remember, Excel proficiency is a step-by-step process, and the knowledge you're gaining now will be the foundation for more advanced concepts in the chapters that follow.

Next up, in Chapter 4, we'll dive into the world of data entry and formatting, crucial skills for any Excel user.

Chapter 4: Data Entry and Formatting

In this chapter, we explore the fundamental aspects of data entry and formatting in Microsoft Excel. Efficiently entering data and presenting it in a structured and visually appealing manner is essential for making the most of this powerful spreadsheet tool.

4.1 Data Entry

Excel's primary purpose is to help you organize and manipulate data. Here's how to enter data into a worksheet:

1.   Select a Cell: Click on the cell where you want to enter data. The selected cell is outlined, and its address appears in the Name Box.

2.   Type Data: Start typing your data. You can enter numbers, text, dates, and more. Press "Enter" when you're done to move to the next cell.

3.   Navigating Cells: Use the arrow keys on your keyboard to move around cells. The "Tab" key moves you to the cell on the right, and "Enter" moves you down to the cell below.

4.   Editing Data: To edit data, double-click the cell or press "F2." You can also edit in the Formula Bar.

4.2 Formatting Data

Formatting your data is key to improving readability and conveying information effectively. Here are some essential formatting options:

• Font Formatting: Use the options in the Home tab to change font type, size, color, and style. Make text bold, italic, or underlined as needed.

• Cell Alignment: The alignment options allow you to control how text is positioned within a cell. You can align text to the left, center, or right and adjust vertical alignment.

• Number Formatting: Excel provides a wide range of number formats, from general to currency, percentage, date, and more. Apply the appropriate format to your data.

• Cell Borders and Fill: Add cell borders to create tables, and use fill color to highlight specific cells. This is particularly useful for emphasizing important data.

• Cell Styles: Excel offers predefined cell styles for tables, headers, and more. You can select a style that suits your data presentation.

4.3 Data Validation

Data validation is a powerful feature in Excel that helps ensure the accuracy and consistency of your data. You can set rules that define what can be entered in a cell. For example, you can limit data to a certain range, require unique values, or use a custom formula to validate input.

To set up data validation:

1.   Select the cell or cells where you want to apply data validation.

2.   Go to the Data tab.

3.   Click on "Data Validation" and define your rules.

4.4 Wrapping Text

Sometimes, the data you want to display is too long to fit

within a single cell. Excel allows you to wrap text within a cell so that it's displayed on multiple lines, making it easier to read.

To wrap text in a cell:

1.   Select the cell.

2.   Go to the Alignment group in the Home tab.

3.   Click on the "Wrap Text" button.

4.5 AutoFill

Excel offers the AutoFill feature, which is handy for quickly populating cells with a series of data. For example, you can autofill a series of numbers, dates, or even custom lists.

To use AutoFill:

1. Enter the first item in a cell.

2. Place your cursor at the lower-right corner of the cell (a small square appears).

3. Drag the square downward or to the right to autofill adjacent cells.

4.6 Your Progress

As you master data entry and formatting in Excel, you're building a strong foundation for using this software effectively. These skills are essential for creating organized and visually appealing spreadsheets, whether for personal or professional use.

In Chapter 5, we'll delve into the world of basic formulas and functions, which will enable you to perform calculations and manipulate your data in powerful ways. Remember that Excel proficiency is a gradual process, and each chapter equips you with new skills that will contribute to your growing expertise.

Next, we explore the power of formulas and functions in Chapter 5.

Chapter 5: Basic Formulas and Functions

In this chapter, we venture into the heart of Excel's capabilities: formulas and functions. These tools empower you to perform calculations, manipulate data, and unlock the full potential of your spreadsheets.

5.1 Formulas: The Building Blocks

Formulas in Excel are expressions that instruct the program to perform calculations based on the data in your worksheets. A formula typically starts with an equals sign (=) and can include cell references, operators, and functions. Here are some basic formula elements:

• Cell References: You can refer to other cells in your formula using their addresses. For example, "=A1+B1" adds the values in cells A1 and B1.

• Operators: Excel supports various operators, such as + (addition), - (subtraction), * (multiplication), and / (division). You can use these to perform mathematical operations.

• Functions: Functions are pre-built formulas designed for specific tasks. Excel offers a wide range of functions, from simple ones like SUM and AVERAGE to more complex ones for statistical analysis and database operations.

5.2 Common Functions

Let's explore a few of the most common functions that you'll frequently use:

• SUM: This function adds up a range of

numbers. For instance, "=SUM(A1:A5)" calculates the sum of values in cells A1 to A5.

- AVERAGE: AVERAGE computes the average of a set of numbers. "=AVERAGE(B1:B5)" gives you the average of values in cells B1 to B5.

- MAX and MIN: MAX returns the largest number in a range, while MIN returns the smallest. "=MAX(C1:C5)" will find the highest value in cells C1 to C5.

- COUNT: COUNT counts the number of cells in a range that contain numbers. "=COUNT(D1:D5)" would count the cells with numerical values in the range D1 to D5.

- IF: The IF function allows you to perform conditional calculations. For example, "=IF(E1>10, "Yes", "No")" checks if the value in cell E1 is greater than 10 and returns "Yes" if true, and "No" if false.

5.3 Writing Formulas

To write a formula in Excel, follow these steps:

1.   Select the cell where you want the result to appear.

2.   Start by typing an equals sign (=).

3.   Enter your formula using cell references, operators, and functions.

4.   Press "Enter" to complete the formula. The cell will display the result.

5.4 Copying Formulas

Excel makes it easy to copy and apply formulas to multiple cells. To do this:

1.   Click on the cell containing the formula you

want to copy.

2.   Position your cursor at the lower-right corner of the cell (the fill handle).

3.   Drag the fill handle to adjacent cells where you want to apply the formula. Excel will adjust cell references automatically.

5.5 Error Handling

Mistakes can happen when writing formulas. Excel provides error-checking tools to help you identify and correct errors. Common errors include:

•   #DIV/0!: Occurs when you try to divide by zero.

•   #VALUE!: Appears when there is an issue with data types.

•   #NAME?: Occurs when Excel doesn't

recognize a function or formula.

Excel provides suggestions and options for correcting these errors, making it easier to troubleshoot and refine your formulas.

5.6 Your Formula Toolbox

As you delve into the world of formulas and functions, you're gaining the tools to perform calculations and manipulate data in Excel. These are invaluable skills whether you're managing finances, analyzing data, or creating reports.

In Chapter 6, we'll take your Excel journey further by exploring how to manage worksheets and workbooks effectively. Remember that mastering Excel is a gradual process, and each chapter equips you with new skills that contribute to your growing expertise.

Next, we'll focus on managing worksheets and workbooks in Chapter 6.

Chapter 6: Managing Worksheets and Workbooks

In this chapter, we shift our focus to the organization and management of worksheets and workbooks in Microsoft Excel. Understanding how to efficiently work with multiple sheets and files is essential for handling complex projects and data.

6.1 Adding, Renaming, and Deleting Worksheets

Excel allows you to work with multiple worksheets within a single workbook. You can add, rename, and delete worksheets as needed:

• Adding Worksheets: To add a new worksheet, click the "+" button located to the right of the sheet tabs at the bottom of the Excel window. A new sheet will be created.

• Renaming Worksheets: Double-click on the sheet tab to rename it. Give your worksheets meaningful names to keep your project organized.

• Deleting Worksheets: To remove a worksheet, right-click on the sheet tab, select "Delete," and confirm your choice.

6.2 Moving and Copying Worksheets

Excel enables you to move or copy worksheets within the same workbook or to other workbooks. This is particularly useful for reorganizing data or sharing specific sections of your project:

• Moving Worksheets: To move a worksheet,

right-click on the sheet tab, select "Move or Copy," choose the destination within the current workbook, and click "OK."

• Copying Worksheets: To copy a worksheet, follow the same process as moving, but select "Create a copy" before clicking "OK."

6.3 Grouping Worksheets

Grouping worksheets can be beneficial when you want to apply changes to multiple sheets simultaneously. For example, you can group sheets to enter the same data or formatting in all of them at once:

1.   Hold down the "Ctrl" key.

2.   Click on the sheet tabs you want to group.

3.   Release the "Ctrl" key. You'll see that the selected sheets are grouped together.

Remember to ungroup sheets when you're done to avoid unintended changes to other sheets.

6.4 Protecting Worksheets and Workbooks

Data security is a crucial consideration in Excel. You can protect your worksheets and workbooks with passwords to restrict access or editing. Here's how:

- Protecting Worksheets: Go to the Review tab, select "Protect Sheet," and set a password. You can specify what actions are allowed on the protected sheet.

- Protecting Workbooks: To protect the entire workbook, use "Protect Workbook" under the Review tab. This secures the structure and windows of the workbook.

6.5 Managing Multiple Workbooks

In addition to managing worksheets, you might need to work with multiple Excel files. Here's how to navigate between open workbooks and manage them efficiently:

• Switching Between Workbooks: Click on the workbook name in the Windows group on the View tab to switch between open workbooks.

• Viewing Multiple Workbooks: Arrange multiple workbooks on your screen using options like "Arrange All" or "View Side by Side" under the View tab.

6.6 Your Excel Toolkit Grows

By understanding how to manage worksheets and workbooks in Excel, you're enhancing your ability to handle complex projects and data. These skills are particularly valuable in professional settings where data management and organization are key.

In Chapter 7, we'll delve into data visualization with charts, allowing you to present your data in a compelling and informative way. Each chapter adds another layer to your Excel expertise, bringing you closer to mastering this versatile software.

Next, we explore the world of charts and graphs in Chapter 7.

Chapter 7: Data Visualization with Charts

In this chapter, we transition from data management to data presentation. Excel offers a powerful set of tools for visualizing your data through charts and graphs. Whether you're summarizing trends, comparing data, or highlighting key insights, charts can make your data come to life.

7.1 The Power of Data Visualization

Data visualization is the art of representing data graphically to make it easier to understand and analyze. Here's why it's important:

• Clarity: Charts simplify complex data, allowing you to spot trends, patterns, and outliers at a glance.

• Communication: Charts make it easier to convey information to others, whether it's in a report, presentation, or a simple data summary.

• Decision-Making: Visualizing data helps in making informed decisions based on a clear understanding of the information.

7.2 Types of Excel Charts

Excel offers a variety of chart types, each suited for specific data and visualization needs. Common chart types include:

• Column Chart: Ideal for comparing values across categories.

- Bar Chart: Like column charts, but with horizontal bars.

- Line Chart: Useful for showing trends over time.

- Pie Chart: Shows the contribution of parts to a whole.

- Area Chart: Similar to a line chart but shaded to emphasize the area beneath the line.

- Scatter Plot: Visualizes the relationship between two sets of data.

- Radar Chart: Displays data in a circular pattern, useful for comparing multiple data points.

- Histogram: Represents the distribution of a dataset.

7.3 Creating Charts in Excel

To create a chart in Excel, follow these general steps:

1. Select the data you want to chart.

2. Go to the Insert tab.

3. Choose the chart type that best fits your data.

4. Excel will create the chart based on your selection.

You can further customize your chart by adding titles, labels, and adjusting its appearance.

7.4 Formatting and Customizing Charts

Excel provides numerous options for formatting and customizing your charts. You can change colors, fonts, and add various elements such as data labels, gridlines, and legends.

Customization allows you to make your chart visually appealing and convey your message effectively.

7.5 Updating and Modifying Charts

Data changes over time, and your charts should reflect these changes. To update a chart:

1. Click on the chart.

2. Go to the Chart Tools tab.

3. Use the "Select Data" or "Edit Data" option to modify the chart's data source.

This flexibility ensures your charts remain accurate and relevant.

7.6 Your Data Comes to Life

With an understanding of chart creation and customization, you're equipped to visually represent your data in meaningful ways. This skill is valuable for professionals, students, and anyone seeking to convey information effectively.

In Chapter 8, we dive into sorting and filtering data in Excel. These techniques are crucial for organizing and extracting specific information from your spreadsheets. Your journey to Excel mastery continues with each chapter, bringing you closer to becoming a proficient user.

Next, we explore the world of sorting and filtering in Chapter 8.

Chapter 8: Sorting and Filtering Data

In this chapter, we explore the vital techniques of sorting and filtering data in Microsoft Excel. These operations allow you to organize, analyze, and extract specific information from your spreadsheets, making your data more meaningful and actionable.

8.1 Why Sort and Filter Data

Sorting and filtering are indispensable for data management. Here's why they matter:

- Data Organization: Sorting helps arrange data

in a meaningful order, making it easier to spot trends and patterns.

• Data Extraction: Filtering allows you to display specific subsets of data, helping you focus on what's relevant to your analysis or task.

• Efficiency: Sorting and filtering tools help you work more efficiently, particularly with large datasets.

8.2 Sorting Data

Excel offers a simple way to sort your data based on one or multiple columns. To sort data:

1. Select the range of cells you want to sort.

2. Go to the Data tab.

3. Click on the "Sort A to Z" or "Sort Z to A" buttons to sort in ascending or descending order.

You can also perform custom sorts, such as sorting by date or text length.

8.3 Filtering Data

Filtering allows you to display only the data that meets specific criteria. To filter data:

1.   Select the range you want to filter.

2.   Go to the Data tab.

3.   Click on the "Filter" button.

This adds filter arrows to your column headers. You can use these arrows to specify filter criteria, such as showing values greater than a certain number or containing specific text.

8.4 Advanced Filtering

Excel's filtering capabilities go beyond basic criteria. You can apply advanced filters to extract more complex datasets. For instance, you can filter for unique records, use logical operators (AND, OR), and create custom criteria.

8.5 Clearing Filters

To remove filters and show all data again:

1.   Click on the filter arrow in any filtered column.

2.   Choose "Clear Filter."

This action clears all filters in the worksheet.

8.6 Data Sorting and Filtering Best Practices

• Use meaningful column headers: Clear and descriptive column headers make sorting and filtering more intuitive.

• Keep a backup: Before sorting or filtering, consider making a backup copy of your data in case you need to revert to the original.

• Be consistent: Consistency in data entry and formatting simplifies sorting and filtering processes.

8.7 Your Data, Your Way

With the knowledge of sorting and filtering, you have the power to transform a vast dataset into actionable insights. Whether you're organizing information, extracting specific details, or spotting trends, these techniques are essential for efficient data management.

In Chapter 9, we delve into the world of data analysis in Excel, covering essential tools and functions for deeper insights. Your journey to Excel mastery continues with each chapter, equipping you with valuable skills for various applications.

Chapter 9: Introduction to Data Analysis

In this chapter, we delve into the world of data analysis in Microsoft Excel. Data analysis is a critical component of Excel's functionality, allowing you to uncover insights, identify trends, and make informed decisions based on your data.

9.1 The Importance of Data Analysis

Data analysis is the process of inspecting, cleaning, transforming, and modeling data to discover useful information, draw conclusions, and support decision-making. Here's why data analysis is crucial:

• Informed Decision-Making: Data analysis provides insights that can guide decisions, whether in business, research, or personal life.

• Detecting Patterns and Trends: Analysis helps identify patterns and trends in your data that might not be apparent at first glance.

• Quality Assurance: Data analysis can reveal errors or inconsistencies in your data that need to be addressed.

• Optimizing Processes: Analyzing data can lead to process improvements, cost reductions, and increased efficiency.

9.2 Data Analysis Tools in Excel

Excel provides a variety of tools for data analysis, including:

- PivotTables: PivotTables are used to summarize and analyze data from large datasets. They allow you to reorganize and group data for a better understanding of your information.

- Data Tables: Data Tables help you perform sensitivity analysis, which involves changing input values in your calculations to see how they affect the results.

- Solver: Solver is an Excel add-in that allows you to solve optimization and simulation problems. It's particularly useful for making decisions when there are multiple variables involved.

- Goal Seek: Goal Seek is a built-in tool for finding the input value needed to achieve a specific result in a formula.

- Analysis ToolPak: The Analysis ToolPak is an Excel add-in that provides a wide range of data analysis tools, including regression, sampling, and descriptive statistics.

9.3 Using PivotTables

PivotTables are a powerful tool for summarizing and analyzing data. To create a PivotTable:

1.   Select the data you want to analyze.

2.   Go to the Insert tab.

3.   Click on "PivotTable" and choose the location for the PivotTable.

4.   Drag and drop fields to the PivotTable Fields area to arrange and summarize your data.

9.4 Data Tables and Goal Seek

Data Tables and Goal Seek are valuable for performing sensitivity analysis. Data Tables allow you to explore how changing input values affect a formula's results. Goal Seek lets you determine the input needed to achieve a specific outcome.

9.5 Solver: Optimizing Solutions

Solver is an advanced tool used to find the best solution for a problem that involves multiple variables. It's commonly used in finance, operations research, and engineering to optimize various scenarios.

9.6 Your Data Analysis Journey

With an introduction to data analysis tools in Excel, you've taken the first steps towards deriving insights from your data. Data analysis is a vital skill for professionals in various fields, and Excel provides the tools to make this process accessible and efficient.

In Chapter 10, we'll explore various tips and tricks to improve your efficiency and productivity in Excel. As you progress through the chapters, your Excel skills become more versatile, setting the stage for you to become a proficient user.

Chapter 10: Excel Efficiency Tips and Tricks

In this chapter, we'll explore various tips and tricks to enhance your efficiency and productivity while working in Microsoft Excel. Mastering these techniques will help you become a more proficient and effective Excel user.

10.1 Keyboard Shortcuts

Keyboard shortcuts are a fast way to perform common tasks without navigating through menus. Here are a few essential keyboard shortcuts:

- Ctrl + C: Copy selected cells.

- Ctrl + X: Cut selected cells.

- Ctrl + V: Paste copied or cut cells.

- Ctrl + Z: Undo the last action.

- Ctrl + Y: Redo an action.

- Ctrl + S: Save your workbook.

- Ctrl + P: Print the current sheet.

- Ctrl + F: Open the Find dialog box.

- Ctrl + A: Select all cells in the current sheet.

- Ctrl + Arrow Keys: Navigate to the edge of data in a worksheet.

These shortcuts can significantly speed up your work in Excel.

10.2 AutoFill

AutoFill is a handy feature for quickly populating cells with data. To use AutoFill:

1.   Enter a value or pattern in a cell.

2.   Click and drag the fill handle (the small square at the bottom-right corner of the selected cell) to fill adjacent cells.

Excel will automatically continue the pattern.

10.3 Custom Lists

Excel allows you to create custom lists that you can use with AutoFill. For example, if you have a list of months that you frequently use, you can create a custom list and use AutoFill to populate your data.

To create a custom list:

1.   Go to the File tab.

2.   Click on Options.

3.   Under the Advanced category, scroll down to the General section.

4.   Click on "Edit Custom Lists."

10.4 Data Validation

Data validation is a powerful tool for ensuring data accuracy and consistency. You can define rules that limit what can be entered in a cell. To set up data validation:

1.   Select the cell or cells where you want to apply data validation.

2.   Go to the Data tab.

3.   Click on "Data Validation" and specify your

criteria.

10.5 Using Named Ranges

Named ranges make it easier to work with data in Excel. Instead of referring to cells by their addresses, you can use meaningful names. To create a named range:

1. Select the range of cells.

2. Go to the Formulas tab.

3. Click on "Define Name."

Named ranges can improve the readability of your formulas.

10.6 Conditional Formatting

Conditional formatting allows you to highlight specific cells based on their content. For example, you can highlight all values above a certain threshold in a different color. To use conditional formatting:

1. Select the cells you want to format.

2. Go to the Home tab.

3. Click on "Conditional Formatting" and choose your formatting rules.

10.7 Templates and Themes

Excel offers a range of templates and themes to give your workbooks a professional and polished look. You can find templates for budgets, calendars, project plans, and more.

To access templates, go to the File tab and select "New." You can also customize themes to change the look and feel of your workbooks.

10.8 Excel Add-Ins

Excel Add-Ins are additional features and functionalities that you can add to Excel. These can enhance your capabilities in areas like data analysis, data visualization, and more. Explore available Add-Ins to see if any suit your needs.

10.9 Your Proficiency Grows

With these efficiency tips and tricks, you're well on your way to becoming a more proficient Excel user. Excel is a versatile tool, and mastering it involves not only understanding its features but also using them efficiently.

As you continue to explore and apply Excel in your work

and projects, you'll discover even more ways to improve your productivity. Your journey to Excel mastery has equipped you with a wide range of skills for various applications.

Congratulations on reaching the end of this beginner's guide to Excel! Whether you're a student, professional, or hobbyist, Excel offers a world of possibilities for data management, analysis, and visualization. Continue to explore and expand your Excel skills, and you'll find it to be an invaluable tool in your endeavors.

Happy   Excel-ing!

www.ingramcontent.com/pod-product-compliance
Lightning Source LLC
LaVergne TN
LVHW051614050326
832903LV00033B/4488